EP First Reader
Workbook

All-in-One
Homeschool

I'm _____.

This is my workbook. My favorite books are

_____

_____

_____

_____

ISBN-13: 978-1505408249
ISBN-10: 1505408245

Third Edition: February 2018

About This Workbook

This is an offline workbook of vocabulary puzzles and games for Easy Peasy All-in-One Homeschool's reading course for Level 1. We've modified and expanded upon the online activities available at the Easy Peasy All-in-One Homeschool website (www.allinonehomeschool.com) so that your child can work offline if desired. Whether you use the online or offline versions, or a combination of both, your child will enjoy these supplements to the Easy Peasy reading course.

How to Use This Workbook

This workbook is designed to be used as a complement to Easy Peasy's reading curriculum, either the online or offline version. It provides ample activities to help your child master the vocabulary words in Level 1. On any given day, use the Activity List to pick out an activity and have your child work on it. Here's our suggestion:

Use the worksheets with day numbers on the specified days when:
- The online course or EP reader instructs to review the vocabulary words or to play an online vocabulary game.

Use the additional worksheets any time during the course when:
- Your child needs more practice on a specific topic.
- Your child wants extra activities just for fun.

The solutions to selected activities are included at the end of the workbook.

Activity List

Missing Letters

Fill in the missing letters.

	_____an
	_____ed
	_____ee
	_____rog
	_____og

Word Families

Write as many words as you can for each word family.

___AT

___ED

___UN

___IG

Synonyms Bubbles

Synonyms are words that have the same or nearly the same meaning. Color the
bubbles that contain synonyms.

Comparative Chart I

Can you fill in all the clouds?

Adjective	Comparative	Superlative
good	better	
sad		saddest
hairy	hairier	
	nearer	nearest
dark	darker	
	louder	loudest
muddy		muddiest
steep	steeper	
	foggier	foggiest
big	bigger	

Synonyms Matching

Synonyms are words that have the same or nearly the same meaning. Connect the words with their synonyms. (The solution is on page 70.)

angry	beneath
under	correct
dirt	terrible
right	mad
awful	speak
begin	shut
say	soil
close	start

Synonyms Crossword

Synonyms are words that have the same or nearly the same meaning. (The solution is on page 70.)

Across

1. look
3. clever
5. noisy
6. ill
9. shout
10. odor

Down

1. alike
2. street
4. speak
6. little
7. sob
8. quick

Antonyms Bubbles

Antonyms are words that have opposite or nearly opposite meanings. Color the bubbles that contain antonyms.

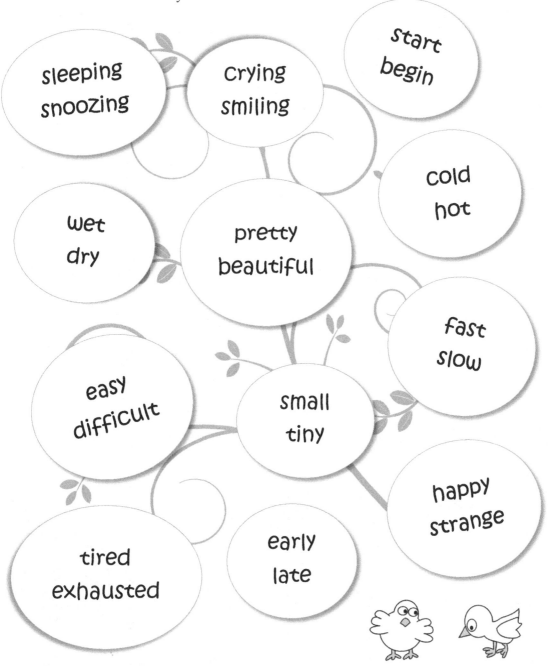

Word Families

Write as many words as you can for each word family.

___AN

___OT

___IN

___AP

Comparative Chart II

Can you put these groups of words in order?

muddy, muddiest, muddier

slimy, slimiest, slimier

more beautiful, most beautiful, beautiful

friendlier, friendly, friendliest

most interesting, interesting, more interesting

Homophones Fill-in-the-Blanks

Homophones are words that sound the same but have different meanings and spellings. Choose the correct homonym for each sentence. (The solution is on page 70.)

---

blue *or* blew?

She made a wish and _____ the candles out.

---

deer *or* dear?

_____ feed on a grass, twigs, and bark.

---

ant *or* aunt?

I visited my _____ last summer.

---

right *or* write?

I think my answers are _____.

---

one *or* won?

My team _____ the game today!

Antonyms Matching

Antonyms are words that have opposite or nearly opposite meanings. Connect the words with their antonyms. (The solution is on page 70.)

day	answer
question	noisy
more	night
remember	easy
difficult	pull
push	less
real	fake
quiet	forget

ABC Order I

Can you put the words in each box in alphabetical order?

fish   cat
paint   tree

1. _____

2. _____

3. _____

4. _____

mob   sand
book   present

1. _____

2. _____

3. _____

4. _____

noisy   fun
game   party

1. _____

2. _____

3. _____

4. _____

frog   rabbit
dog   balloon

1. _____

2. _____

3. _____

4. _____

ABC Order II

Can you put these 10 words in alphabetical order?

map	bee	1.
ape	lamp	2.
friend	kitten	3.
tower	hello	4.
land	zoo	5.
		6.
		7.
		8.
		9.
		10.

Missing Letters I

Fill in the missing letters.

	____heep
	____en
	____ap
	____all
	____at

Missing Letters II

Fill in the missing letters.

	____wl
	____oad
	____pple
	____lower
	____oot

Missing Letters III

Fill in the missing letters.

	____and
	____ood
	____oat
	____ish
	____ree

Missing Letters IV

Fill in the missing letters.

	_____anana
	_____esk
	_____izza
	_____ight
	_____read

Find the Nouns I

Circle the nouns in the box below. The words are from *The Tale of Peter Rabbit.*

root	big	tree	down
garden	accident	there	along
go	umbrella	bunny	gather
naughty	gate	beans	meet
thief	frightened	among	jacket
carefully	door	locked	milk

But Peter, who was very naughty, ran straight away to Mr. McGregor's garden, and squeezed under the gate!
 – *The Tale of Peter Rabbit*

Find the Nouns II

Circle the nouns in the box below. The words are from *The Adventures of Danny Meadow Mouse*.

worst	cousin	habit	toad
drink	clothes	ugly	fellow
fox	tired	sleepy	story
squeaky	dinner	morning	quick
tunnel	snow	breakfast	cruel

All Danny Meadow Mouse could think about was his short tail.
- *The Adventures of Danny Meadow Mouse*

Singular or Plural I

Circle the correct word to complete each sentence.

 She bought two (apple / **apples**).

 A (**mouse** / mice) is running.

 I had three (strawberry / **strawberries**).

 We saw a (**frog** / frogs) in a pond.

 We picked two (flower / **flowers**).

 I can eat three (muffin / **muffins**)!

Singular or Plural II

Circle the singular words in red and the plural words in blue.

knife	books	table	owl
mix	shelf	feet	leaves
cars	mice	cities	tooth
stories	wolf	bike	tales
washes	apple	fox	key
man	toys	boxes	watches

Mrs. Rabbit gives Peter chamomile tea.
- *The Tale of Peter Rabbit*

Plurals Word Search

Find and circle the hidden words. Use your favorite colors. The words can go in any direction, even backwards! (The solution is on page 70.)

```
L  P  F  Q  X  Y  P  K  W  C  K
G  E  S  C  A  R  S  N  A  Y  D
R  J  A  H  A  H  S  I  T  P  X
A  M  L  V  E  N  B  V  C  I  M
B  T  I  W  E  L  G  E  H  U  V
B  X  A  X  O  S  V  S  E  Q  Z
I  P  M  B  E  L  Q  E  S  T  X
T  D  I  J  L  S  V  M  S  O  T
S  H  F  W  O  E  V  E  S  Y  E
I  F  B  I  K  E  S  R  S  S  T
Y  X  W  A  S  H  E  S  I  V  F
```

shelves	watches	bikes	leaves
washes	mixes	tables	rabbits
wolves	knives	cars	toys

Double Letter Spelling I

Can you figure out what same two letters are missing from the words in each group? Can you think of more examples? Use the pictures as hints.

Group 1: r _ _ t   f _ _ t

Group 2:  w _ _ d   f _ _ d

Group 3: s _ _ n      m _ _ n

Group 4: p _ _ r   d _ _ r

Group 5: br _ _ m      bl _ _ m

Double Letter Spelling II

Can you figure out what same two letters are missing from the words in each group? Can you think of more examples? Use the pictures as hints.

Group 1:   s _ _   b _ _

Group 2:   sh _ _ p   sl _ _ p

Group 3:   k _ _ p   p _ _ p

Group 4:   sw _ _ p   st _ _ p

Group 5:   fr _ _   tr _ _

Double Letter Spelling III

Can you figure out what same two letters are missing from the words in each group? Can you think of more examples? Use the pictures as hints.

Group 1: wi _ _  hi _ _

Group 2: bi _ _ pi _ _

Group 3:  dri _ _ fri _ _

Group 4: ba _ _  ca _ _

Group 5: wa _ _ do _ _

Double Letter Spelling IV

Can you figure out what same two letters are missing from the words in each group? Can you think of more examples? Use the pictures as hints.

Group 1:	be _ _ y 	me _ _ y
Group 2:	 che _ _ y	ca _ _ y
Group 3:	cu _ _ y hu _ _ y	
Group 4:	 wo _ _ y	so _ _ y
Group 5:	blu _ _ y flu _ _ y	

Rhyming Words I

Color the bubbles that contain rhyming words.

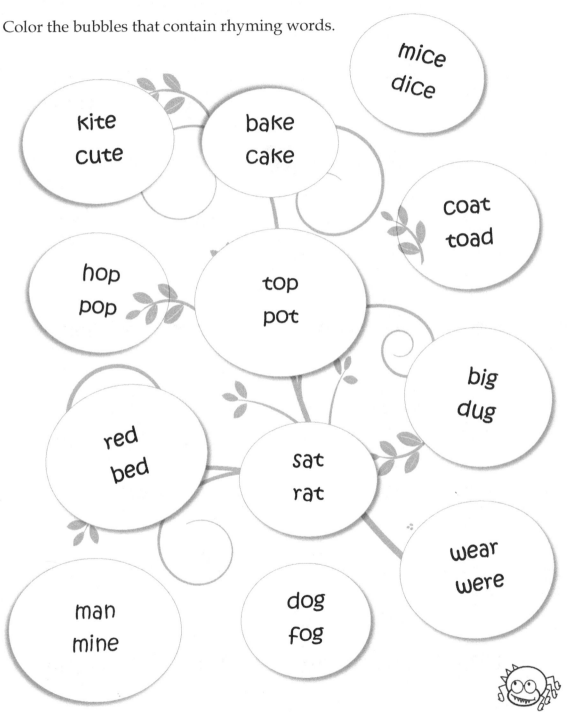

mice
dice

kite
cute

bake
cake

coat
toad

hop
pop

top
pot

big
dug

red
bed

sat
rat

wear
were

man
mine

dog
fog

Rhyming Words II

Circle the word(s) that rhyme with the first word in each row.

pie   lie   cry   field

set   sit   get   bed

cow   pow   now   saw

cat   way   law   bat

wish   fish   shoot   dish

ring   wing   king   sang

Rhyming Words III

Circle the word(s) that rhyme with the first word in each row.

lip	sip	cup	tub
hot	rot	rat	pot
bed	beg	red	fed
rub	rug	cub	rip
feet	foot	meet	fit
pine	pin	time	mine

Word Families I

Write as many words as you can for each word family.

___UT

___ET

___AD

___OP

Word Families II

Write as many words as you can for each word family.

___EN

___UG

___OB

___EE

Word Families III

Write as many words as you can for each word family.

___AY

___AM

___IT

___ALL

Word Family Word Search I

Find and circle the hidden words. Use your favorite colors. The words can go in any direction, even backwards! (The solution is on page 71.)

B	P	C	O	I	R	Q	I	M	E	A
L	I	J	F	E	N	D	S	C	T	K
D	K	G	D	Q	B	H	T	P	F	O
N	E	S	A	T	K	D	A	B	L	N
N	R	L	T	D	L	I	C	T	B	U
I	U	W	S	V	C	G	I	W	E	S
D	S	R	M	H	U	P	J	N	D	P
A	N	E	Y	T	I	T	U	Q	G	D
B	Q	P	A	G	U	F	B	U	N	M
O	H	M	X	J	O	D	E	F	R	A

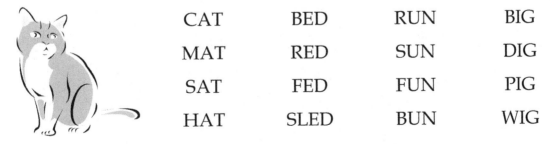

CAT	BED	RUN	BIG
MAT	RED	SUN	DIG
SAT	FED	FUN	PIG
HAT	SLED	BUN	WIG

Word Family Word Search II

Find and circle the hidden words. Use your favorite colors. The words can go in any direction, even backwards! (The solution is on page 71.)

N	A	C	M	P	L	A	O	N	P	P
B	R	A	I	P	H	R	S	I	A	E
J	N	N	A	L	C	J	B	P	C	O
X	C	N	V	F	S	X	P	T	I	U
T	H	I	N	V	K	H	O	T	Q	N
F	F	D	U	G	I	B	S	N	H	M
P	Q	K	A	K	N	Q	G	N	O	I
N	A	W	I	L	T	X	P	A	G	T
S	A	M	S	O	P	D	Y	P	P	Z
D	V	R	P	T	W	B	J	M	D	A

MAN	POT	PIN	GAP
CAN	HOT	THIN	MAP
RAN	NOT	SPIN	CAP
PAN	LOT	SKIN	NAP

Word Family Word Search III

Find and circle the hidden words. Use your favorite colors. The words can go in any direction, even backwards! (The solution is on page 71.)

A	F	D	A	D	B	K	P	E	C	A
T	H	U	P	H	C	S	H	A	J	T
L	E	T	M	O	O	G	H	T	D	E
B	I	A	E	L	P	R	I	U	E	P
F	D	C	Q	B	X	E	Q	D	T	S
L	U	H	C	T	G	V	B	H	N	A
T	D	O	E	K	P	I	K	U	E	L
G	U	G	P	B	O	Y	P	S	Z	B
H	O	P	G	U	M	O	S	A	J	M
J	C	A	T	T	T	V	F	D	W	D

BUT	SET	PAD	POP
CUT	PET	SAD	MOP
HUT	GET	MAD	TOP
PUT	LET	DAD	HOP

Word Family Word Search IV

Find and circle the hidden words. Use your favorite colors. The words can go in any direction, even backwards! (The solution is on page 71.)

T	E	N	J	E	E	R	T	O	B	D
O	C	B	S	I	A	G	U	D	O	T
A	R	E	X	E	S	N	B	S	M	K
L	H	E	R	R	E	O	W	I	F	Y
N	F	T	U	V	C	P	F	E	R	G
M	E	G	K	B	M	B	E	W	J	B
C	P	D	B	Y	N	G	U	M	S	H
B	H	S	C	H	E	W	N	G	V	G
R	O	B	I	U	M	E	X	L	D	N
B	Q	J	Z	G	P	Z	E	R	Q	A

Bumblebee

DEN	MUG	JOB	TREE
MEN	RUG	MOB	SEE
PEN	HUG	COB	BEE
TEN	BUG	ROB	FEE

Word Family Word Search V

Find and circle the hidden words. Use your favorite colors. The words can go in any direction, even backwards! (The solution is on page 72.)

```
J   N   Y   S   A   O   E   S   M   Q   B
T   A   I   H   M   J   W   K   A   L   P
P   T   M   T   E   C   T   Z   X   G   N
R   B   V   B   P   A   Q   I   E   J   R
F   X   A   T   A   L   L   S   B   U   C
O   L   D   A   M   L   W   D   X   H   O
L   W   S   I   V   M   M   Y   A   S   Y
Q   Y   A   M   A   Y   P   T   I   H   J
K   P   A   L   R   A   I   U   F   Z   V
B   Z   S   D   L   B   T   I   N   G   A
```

SAY	DAM	PIT	TALL
DAY	JAM	SIT	WALL
BAY	EXAM	HIT	CALL
PAY	SLAM	BIT	BALL

Word Jumble – Animals I

Unscramble the jumbled words to spell the names of these animals.

E B E

_____

T A C

_____

S F I H

_____

D G O

_____

O A G T

_____

Word Jumble – Animals II

Unscramble the jumbled words to spell the names of these animals.

TADO

_____

IGP

_____

OLW

_____

SEMUO

_____

SPEEH

_____

Word Jumble – Fruits

Unscramble the jumbled words to spell the names of these fruits.

P L E A P

_____

B R Y R E

_____

C R Y E R H

_____

N A N A B A

_____

R P G A E

_____

Word Jumble – Foods

Unscramble the jumbled words to spell the names of these foods.

 M N I F F U

_____

 M J A

_____

 B D E A R

_____

 Z Z I P A

_____

 K C E A

_____

Word Jumble – Nature

Unscramble the jumbled words to spell these things in nature.

N H T I G

_____

O W O D

_____

F W E R L O

_____

O M O N

_____

R E E T

_____

Word Jumble – School

Unscramble the jumbled words to spell these school things.

E N P

_____

L I C P

_____

E S D K

_____

G U E L

_____

B K O O

_____

Word Jumble – Christmas

AGNLE

HLLOY

SATR

SNATA

BLLE

RENIRDEE

CROAL

GFTI

WERATH

SONW

EETR

EFL

_____ _____ _____

_____ _____ _____

_____ _____ _____

_____ _____ _____

Synonyms Matching I

Synonyms are words that have the same or nearly the same meaning. Connect the words with their synonyms. (The solution is on page 72.)

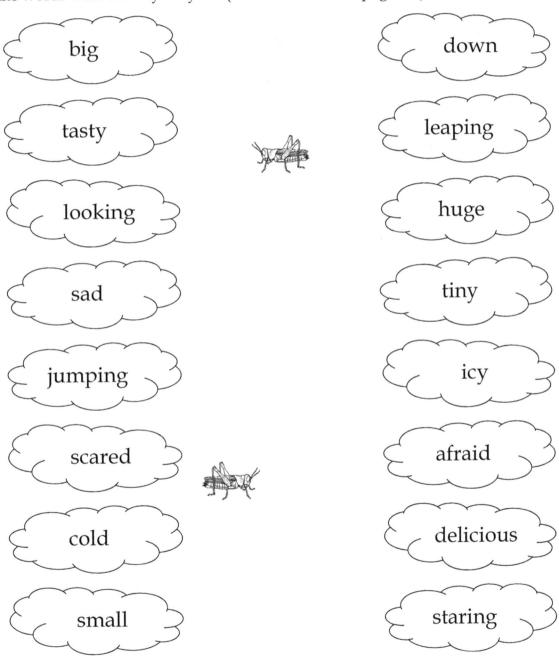

big

down

tasty

leaping

looking

huge

sad

tiny

jumping

icy

scared

afraid

cold

delicious

small

staring

Synonyms Matching II

Synonyms are words that have the same or nearly the same meaning. Write a synonym for each word. (The solution is on page 72.)

JOB   mad   trousers   little   present
eNd   PRETTY   over   street   earth

lovely		
above		
finish		
small		
angry		
pants		
road		
gift		
work		
world		

Synonyms Matching III

Synonyms are words that have the same or nearly the same meaning. Write a synonym for each word. (The solution is on page 72.)

join   SMart   land   wealthy   annoy

Lead   swap   ending   ALIKE   grin

smile		
ground		
same		
bother		
connect		
guide		
clever		
trade		
rich		
conclusion		

Synonyms Matching IV

Synonyms are words that have the same or nearly the same meaning. Write a synonym for the underlined word. (The solution is on page 73.)

angry   QUICKLY   tidy   shut   dirty

speak   RIGHt   start   TERRIBLE   happy

Let's <u>begin</u> the lesson.

_____

The room is <u>messy</u>.

_____

I need to <u>talk</u> with you.

_____

I'm <u>glad</u> to see you.

_____

Your room is very <u>neat</u>.

_____

Please <u>close</u> the door.

_____

I ran as <u>fast</u> as possible.

_____

The smell is <u>awful</u>.

_____

Your answer is <u>correct</u>.

_____

Are you <u>mad</u> at me?

_____

Antonyms Matching I

Antonyms are words that have opposite or nearly opposite meanings. Connect the words with their antonyms. (The solution is on page 73.)

straight

cold

all

right

young

fast

rich

smart

hot

wrong

poor

bent

stupid

slow

old

Antonyms Matching II

Antonyms are words that have opposite or nearly opposite meanings. Write an antonym for each word. (The solution is on page 73.)

FULL   good   far   smile   short

SaMe   SICK   loW   late   doWN

early	
long	
bad	
empty	
up	
healthy	
frown	
different	
high	
near	

Antonyms Matching III

Antonyms are words that have opposite or nearly opposite meanings. Write an antonym for each word. (The solution is on page 73.)

create   dULL   win   exit   buy

top   IGNORE   quiet   FLOAT   small

enter		
large		
destroy		
loud		
listen		
lose		
sink		
shiny		
bottom		
sell		

Antonyms Matching IV

Antonyms are words that have opposite or nearly opposite meanings. Write an antonym for the underlined word. (The solution is on page 73.)

SLOWLY   WET   BACKWARD   stop   last

west   cold   left   DIFFICULT   sunny

Let's <u>begin</u> the lesson.   _____

It's <u>hot</u> today.   _____

The question is <u>easy</u>.   _____

My clothes are <u>dry</u>.   _____

I ran as <u>fast</u> as possible.   _____

This is the <u>first</u> chapter.   _____

The car moved <u>forward</u>.   _____

The sun rises in the <u>east</u>.   _____

The weather is <u>cloudy</u>.   _____

Let's go to the <u>right</u>.   _____

Antonyms Crossword

Antonyms are words that have opposite or nearly opposite meanings. (The solution is on page 74.)

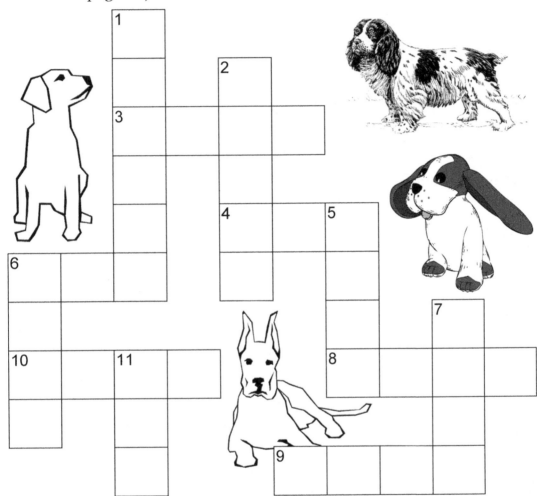

Across

3. odd
4. in
6. wet
8. far
9. right
10. strong

Down

1. ugly
2. above
5. fat
6. up
7. slow
11. subtract

Homophones Fill-in-the-Blanks I

Homophones are words that sound the same but have different meanings and spellings. Choose the correct homonym for each sentence. (The solution is on page 74.)

---

piece *or* peace?

Would you like to have a _____ of pie?

---

whole *or* hole?

He dug a deep _____ with his spade.

---

tail *or* tale?

The dog is wagging his _____.

---

tea or tee?

Would you like a cup of _____?

---

weak *or* week?

He was too _____ to stand.

Homophones Fill-in-the-Blanks II

Homophones are words that sound the same but have different meanings and spellings. Choose the correct homonym for each sentence. (The solution is on page 74.)

---

would *or* wood?

We need more _____ for the fire.

---

bury *or* berry?

She picked a _____ from the bush.

---

by *or* buy?

I arrived at the airport _____ train.

---

here *or* hear?

Can you _____ the noise outside?

---

too *or* two?

She bought _____ much food.

Comparative Chart III

Complete the chart below.

Adjective	Comparative	Superlative
blue		
	sweeter	
	shinier	
		finest
rich		
		oldest
	happier	
clean		
high		
		tallest

Sentence Building I

Which sentence is correct? Circle the correct sentences.

a) we bought an apple.
b) We bought an apple.
c) We bought an apple

a) A mouse is running.
b) A mouse is running
c) a mouse is running.

a) I had three strawberries.
b) I had three strawberries
c) i had three strawberries.

a) i saw a frog jumping into a pond.
b) I saw a frog jumping into a pond
c) I saw a frog jumping into a pond.

a) We picked flowers for mom from the garden
b) We picked flowers for mom from the garden.
c) we picked flowers for mom from the garden

Sentence Building II

Put each group of words together to make a sentence. (The solution is on page 74.)

two   have   you   hands

big   my   very   house   is

ran   a   I   mile

like   I   book   this

I   my   aunt   visited

Sentence Building III

Put each group of words together to make a sentence. (The solution is on page 74.)

barking   the   is   dog   loud

my   in   grandma   lives   Philadelphia

I   the   went   store   to

played   with   baseball   we   them

enjoyed   he   eating   strawberries   the

Solutions to Selected Activities

Page 13

Synonyms Matching

angry – mad
under – beneath
dirt – soil
right – correct
awful – terrible
begin – start
say – speak
close – shut

Page 14

Synonyms Crossword

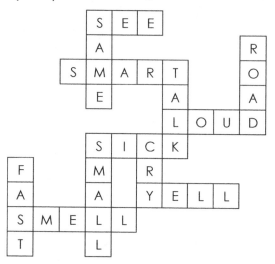

Page 18

Homophones Fill-in-the-Blanks

blew
deer
aunt
right
won

Page 19

Antonyms Matching

day – night
question – answer
more – less
remember – forget
difficult – easy
push – pull
real – fake
quiet – noisy

Page 30

Plurals Word Search

The first letters are marked. Remember that the words can go in any direction!

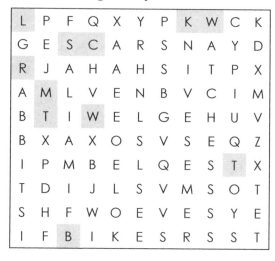

Page 41
Word Family Word Search I

The first letters are marked. Remember that the words can go in any direction!

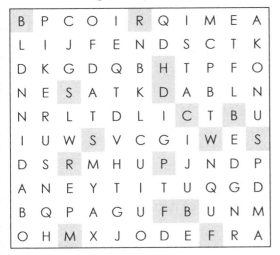

Page 42
Word Family Word Search II

The first letters are marked. Remember that the words can go in any direction!

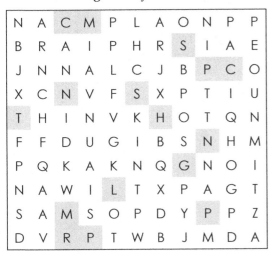

Page 43
Word Family Word Search III

The first letters are marked. Remember that the words can go in any direction!!

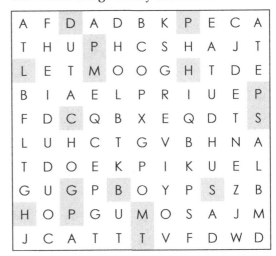

Page 44
Word Family Word Search IV

The first letters are marked. Remember that the words can go in any direction!

Page 45
Word Family Word Search V

The first letters are marked. Remember that the words can go in any direction!

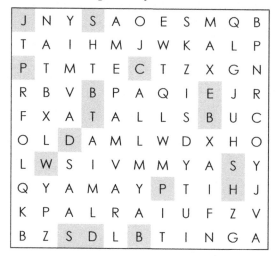

Page 53
Synonyms Matching I

big – huge
tasty – delicious
looking – staring
sad – down
jumping – leaping
scared – afraid
cold – icy
small – tiny

Page 54
Synonyms Matching II

lovely – pretty
above – over
finish – end
small – little
angry – mad
pants – trousers
road – street
gift – present
work – job
world – earth

Page 55
Synonyms Matching III

smile – grin
ground – land
same – alike
bother – annoy
connect – join
guide – lead
clever – smart
trade – swap
rich – wealthy
conclusion – ending

Page 56
Synonyms Matching IV

begin – start
messy – dirty
talk – speak
glad – happy
neat – tidy
close – shut
fast – quickly
awful – terrible
correct – right
mad – angry

Page 57
Antonyms Matching I

straight – bent
cold – hot
all – none
right – wrong
young – old
fast – slow
rich – poor
smart – stupid

Page 58
Antonyms Matching II

early – late
long – short
bad – good
empty – full
up – down
healthy – sick
frown – smile
different – same
high – low
near – far

Page 59
Antonyms Matching III

enter – exit
large – small
destroy – create
loud – quiet
listen – ignore
lose – win
sink – float
shiny – dull
bottom – top
sell – buy

Page 60
Antonyms Matching IV

begin – stop
hot – cold
easy – difficult
dry – wet
fast – slowly
first – last
forward – backward
east – west
cloudy – sunny
right – left

Page 61
Antonyms Crossword

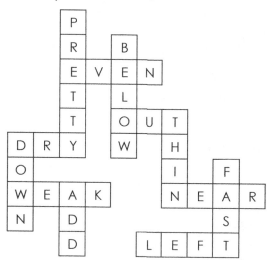

Page 62
Homophones Fill-in-the-Blanks I

piece
hole
tail
tea
weak

Page 63
Homophones Fill-in-the-Blanks II

wood
berry
by
hear
too

Page 66
Sentence Building II

You have two hands.
My house is very big.
I ran a mile.
I like this book.
I visited my aunt.

Page 67
Sentence Building III

The dog is barking loud.
My grandma lives in Philadelphia.
I went to the store.
We played baseball with them.
He enjoyed eating the strawberries.

Made in the USA
Columbia, SC
17 July 2020